Waiting for the blue

To Lee,

thankyou so much for having me on your show, was an absolute pleasure, really appreciate your kind words and support,

take care,
Beth x

29/1/24.

To my friends old and new – you know who you are! – and to my family, who have put up with me the longest! - thank you for walking with me, for your love and support without which I wouldn't have got this far.

To anyone who has ever loved and lost. Who has felt alone, afraid or like the biggest battle to be won is just to get out of bed and face another day. To the fringe dwellers, to those who feel like they don't always belong or that home isn't always the place it should be. To the broken, the breaking, the healing, the changing – I see you. You are not alone.

May this book reach out like a comforting hug to you on those dark days and nights when your emotions feel too much to bear.

To the bravest woman I know. I am blessed to call you a friend - to Claire – your poetry is a beautiful reflection of your soul, keep sharing your light with the world.

Lastly, for my mum – you will always be my whole world and everything in it xxx

Lots of love,
Beth xxx

Contents

Searching

Find me in the storm 2
Hero 3
Hope 6
Park of dreams 8
Searching for Spring 10
Stop reading my diary 11
Waiting for the blue 14

Falling

Burnt out 20
HELP ME 21
I am afraid 22
In your arms 23
Jump out 24
Missing 25
Ocean waves 26
Paradise 28
Pretending 29

Some feelings 31
The girl 33
Way out 35
What would you do? 37
You were well once 38

Friendship

Birthday message 42
Burden 45
Compassionate friend 47
Glimpse of a rainbow 48
Home 49
It's okay 53
Meet up 56
Poetry 58
The rose 60
Thank you 62
The garden 64
The lantern 65
Your voice 68

Goodbye

The last goodbye 73
The promise 76
You're asleep now 80

Reflection

Christmas 82
It's mum's birthday today 84
Long after the flowers had drooped 85
Sorry for your loss 86
The Joker 88
Unexpected friend 91
Wanting 93

The Journey

Bloom again 96
Final journey 97
Found 98
Hopeful eyes 100
I can't explain 101
Oceans blue 102

The nest..104
The scene 107
The test 109

Beyond

Always 111
Enough..113
Love that never breaks............................115
Midnight star..117
My everything 118
Peace 119
Heaven 120

Searching

Find me in the storm

when everything's a mess
When life turns on its head
and you're far from your best.

Find me in the quiet.
In the tranquil evening air
When you close your eyes
I will meet you there.

Find me at my gravestone
I'll watch you sitting by
I'll listen to your love for me
Know it's okay to cry.

I will never leave you
I'm always sitting near
Just call me and I'll rise
Inside your heart I'm always here.

A Hero

A hero isn't someone
who never falls down
A hero is someone
who gets back up off the ground

I want to see you suffer
I want to see you weak
I want to see you struggle
I want to know it's not just me

I don't care if your superpower
can help you lift fifty sheds
My superpower
is getting out of bed

I battle every day
with the monsters in my head
the claws that rip me down
You fight fictional ones instead

I don't care if you are
the strongest man in town
How does that help me?
You don't even notice when I drown

I can't rely on a superhero
to fix the mess of my life
All anyone has is themselves
but no one sees it in that light

No one's going to save you
if you don't try to save yourself
You keep waiting for a hero
you're never going to be helped

So what if you can fly
or keeping holding your breath?
Nothing can release you
from the inevitability of death

You want real superpowers?
My best friend can read my mind
She can see my suffering
when the rest of the world is blind

I can be invisible
it's called not reaching out
it's called keeping quiet
making any doubt

That anything could be
anything but okay
fade into nothing
slip silently away

Trying to play the hero
trying to be tough
trying to take it on the chin
feel never good enough

Everybody suffers
Everybody hurts
Everybody struggles
Pretending not to, is worse

What happens to the heroes
who are too afraid to cry?
All the unshed tears
the suicide rates don't lie.

I don't need a hero
I don't need a special power
I just need a good friend
to sit with me for an hour

Or two, however long it takes
So if you're still looking for a hero
I warn you it's a mistake.

Hope

Wanting to live
but not knowing how
or when or where
keep safe for now

How long will it last
Does anybody know?
Hope in uncertainty
When can we go?

And be free
from our fear
such a difficult year

And yet
we must learn
to live
In times of doubt
in times of friendship
and times without

The closeness of a friend
the people we love
all things, must end

And yet
as a flickering candle
refuses to go out
the whisper of hope
when no hope is about

The refusal to surrender
like a paper boat
adrift on the ocean
still keeping afloat

Hope. That foolish notion.
Hope. Keeps us floating in the ocean.
Hope. When many have drowned.
Hope. Yet still a whisper.
Hope. Will find its own solid ground.

Park of dreams

The song upon the breeze
the whispers in the air
the symphony of nature
its melodies are fair

Rust coloured leaves
carpeting the floor
The rustling sound of autumn
receives a warm encore

Invisible strings
strung against the sun
As autumn falls away
Winter has begun

The icy frost bestows
Nature with white gown
A perfect ring of snowflakes
forms a silver crown

The flowers come out of hiding
the trees are waking up
the ice begins its melting
the babble returns to brook

Light dancing through the trees
upon every leaf it does catch
Sparks of emerald and jade
its brilliant hues unmatched

As spring comes bursting forth
with fresh young shoots anew
searching for summer skies
the perfect shade of blue

Beneath the tangled tree
the lullabies of streams
send me drifting away
in this park of dreams.

Searching for Spring

In the depths of the snow
the snowdrop will open
the crocus will grow

The leaves will return
the roots have survived
No matter how bitter the frost
Spring always revives

Stop reading my diary

Will you please take that out?
Like airing dirty laundry
you know what it's about

Another phrase from my mind
you know what's in my brain
as though you've plucked out my weirdness
we're on the same crazy train

Your words inspire me
ideas take shape and converge
imagery fills my head
as metaphors emerge

How you have the bravery
to stand up in front of a group
I'm just too wimpish
I'd let my confidence stoop

Your voice fills the air
and takes me far away
I've crossed into another realm
my mind it goes astray

How you have the courage
to lay your feelings bare
raw emotion, passion pours out
as I'm listening from the chair

I feel as though I'm with you
I'm going through your mind
I'm flicking through the photographs
I've reached through your insides

You've opened up your heart
blade sliced right through your chest
You've pulled out the largest thorn
and you've laid your woes to rest

How do you manage
to stop from bleeding out?
There's a gaping hole
why don't you just shout?

A silver thread flows
gently across your skin
a steady stream of words
starts to be sewn in

You turned your pain into poetry
your hurt into art
your weakness into courage
sewed up the pieces of your heart

One day I'll be like you
I'll stand up in the crowd
I'll begin to release my thoughts
I'll dare to speak out loud

For now I'm still just thinking
sat writing this poem
One day I'll read it to you
to you I will owe it.

Waiting for the blue

This poem was written as a personal response to someone who appeared to be saying the worst thing about Covid was moving back in with their parents. Whilst I appreciate this can be a difficult thing, I was simply angry at them and the world at the time for not noticing my own overwhelming grief. I am not in any way trying to undermine the experience of others who had suffered immensely during that difficult time and indeed continue to be affected by it. Back then I was simply angry at them for being so hopeful that things would be better and quite blinded by my own loss. Like most of my poems this dialogue was kept in my head until now.

You're waiting for the blue
But I'm not there yet
You talk of hope
as though it's true
but I can't share it

You think we'll build back new
come back better
come back strong
We thought that after World War Two
look how we were wrong

Yes, there were good years
of jubilance and joy
They threw VE day parties
but like a discarded toy

We crept back into our old ways
left our toys out in the rain
Once treasured gifts
now just forgotten all the same

Don't talk to me of hope
when I'm fixed into this winter
like a stinging thorn
I can't take out the splinter

So large, if I take it then I'll die
I'd rather be impaled
have a knife stuck in my eye

I know I'm sounding dramatic but
how can you talk to me of hope
like things will be better?
My mom is *dead*.
I could do nothing to protect her

So many people have died
and the world mourns their loss
Her body lies in the grave
but does the world give a toss?

Lockdown's affected you
I'm sorry I don't care
I'm locked in my grief
too great a burden to bear

Everyone's lost and lonely
wondering what life means
I am broken and not the only
one though to me it seems

I haven't lived in this world
through Covid 2020
My mind's been elsewhere
my bed has been left empty

I've slept on the floor
or rather left wide awake
waiting for the last breath
I don't want to hear her take

You talk of hope
like it's something to be had
like a sick twisted joke
you think things will never again be as bad

How are you so naive
when the world is full of loss?
The next tidal wave will come
and what will be the cost

Next time
will you survive it then?
Will a nice little poem
flow from the ink in your pen?

Damn all the poets
Great writers and thinkers
you live in a dream
your eyes wearing blinkers

What a hypocrite
the antithesis of hope
I sit and write a poem
based on the words you spoke

If I could speak to you now
I think I'd simply scream
I haven't lived in your world
I don't dream the things you dream

I dream that I'm drowning
quickly learn there's no way out
I dream to never wake up
Can you hear me shout?

I must be silent
now is the time to listen
as you share your craft
the air around you glistens

Everyone is spell bound
I'm sat here frustrated
looked forward to your show
for a while I'd waited

Don't talk to me of hope
Don't pretend it will be okay
You may be thoughtful and funny
But I'd wish you'd go away

Right now, I don't think
I'll ever find the blue
Skies of hope shining bright
But if I do, *I will find you.*

Falling

Burnt out

I am exhausted.
Every day I'm burnt out.
The energy I try to mount
but fail, even my sleep
has no relief

Filled with nightmares
broken by helping you
out of bed, or into your chair
I don't want you to think that I don't care

It's not that I don't love you
of course, you know I do
It's just that I'm too tired
to tell you the truth

I'm not as capable as you think
I'm not as strong as you believe
I can't just keep going on, I just need
a break, a good night's rest

And I know you do too
it's far worse for you
Every time you sleep
every time that you do

There's a chance you'll take
one last drink from your cup
One night you'll go to bed
and never wake up.

Help me

Hi, how's it going? You free to chat?
Evening okay? Let's go with that
Let's go for food. Nice place I'll find
Perhaps yes... But perhaps another time

Maybe tomorrow, or the week after next
Eventually next month, did you not get my texts?

I am afraid

to see you in person
my guard will fall away
I know it will for certain

I am afraid
for you to take another look
for you to see, I'm not okay
my anchor's become unstuck

I am afraid
to let myself be sad
because I know I can't stop
Will it always feel this bad?

I am afraid
for you to see, just how broken I am
I just want to be hugged
to feel okay more than I am

I am afraid
of my feelings being made known
and now that's she's nearly gone
I'm afraid of being on my own.

In your arms

You held me in your arms
You loved me from day one
You would hold me in my arms
Until your love was gone.

Jump out

of your brain
It's insane
but I feel
so alive
when I finally
stop trying
stop thinking
just being

Take me to that place
nothing to face
but freedom
Are you scared?

How do I get there?
Does anyone know?
Can anyone tell me
where I can go?

To be free
Just me
Alone
with myself

My thoughts
blown away.
Take me to
a better day.

Missing

I miss being loved
I miss just being hugged
I miss hearing her laugh
Miss the things I can't get back

I miss her advice
her saying things that were nice
Her words always fair
as she gently combed my hair

I miss her warmth
from the day I was born
Her kind eyes, her smile
I miss her all the while

I miss her every single day
The memories they stay
but she's still very much gone
What's left missing the most
is my way to live on.

The ocean waves

seem nice from afar.
Innocent enough
as a rainbow
or a shooting star

But the closer I get
the further I want to run.
Move. Anything
to not become
stuck in the sand.

As the waves rise. Crash.
I fall.
Sink further.
Grasp at nothing at all.

Choking. Can't breathe.
Waves flowing, I seethe
current crushing
around my neck.

My throat.
No sign
of any
lifeboat
Scream won't come out.
Falling. Drowning.
Not able to shout.

Deeper. Deeper.
Lost and forgotten

right at the bottom
of the ocean
of despair
of my mind
swept in the tides
until I
      fall
           asleep.

Paradise

How far away is hell?
It often seems quite near
It's under every heavy breath
attached to every tear

How far away is death?
It's surrounding us now
It's flexing its hand
ready to close just now

The unspoken truth
lingers in the air
Waiting for the inevitable
to rise from the empty chair

This endless suffering
don't think they've got it right
To live is to endure
To die is paradise.

Pretending

I'm tired of pretending to be happy
When I don't understand the feeling
Might give you a smile yet
hope my eyes aren't revealing

Like watching a programme on TV
but it's stuck on mute
I'm trying to understand
but I just can't compute

Think there's far too many
mannequins all in one store
then I notice them move
and walk across the floor

When everyone seems fake
perhaps it's me who's not real
What lies behind the mask?
What am I hoping to conceal?

Searching for normality
when I'm not going to find it
not recognising my name
though I've already signed it

My name is who I am
but there's a piece of me that's missing
I'm only half a person
can't stop myself from wishing

Whenever I return home
as soon as I get through the door
I could give you a hug
but can no longer hug you anymore

I'm not really sure
if I'll ever find normal
at least not the way it was
now everything's abnormal

At least when I sleep
she sometimes visits in my dreams
It's just when I wake up
when nothing is what it seems

Some feelings

There are some feelings
just too big to face
it's never the right time
or ever the right place

There's never a convenient
time to be sad
to cry, to feel lost
or even to be glad

To remember
the kind of woman she was
full of grace, compassion
and always full of love

The mother who knew
she could never leave me
from whose warm gentle spirit
I'd never wish to be free

But the time came
when she finally did.
The world became darker
I simply ran and hid.

Abandoned. Afraid.
There's no way out
being trapped in a cave
I'd much rather be now

Than this cage of depression
grief a noose around my neck
the chains that prevent me
from taking another step

I'm shackled to this pain
Do you see it in my face?
I'm carrying my loss
to yet another place.

The girl

There was a girl
so very small
wretched, ragged
hardly there at all

Every day
prodded and poked
she was tortured
did nothing to provoke

The hot pokers
iron bars
clanging metal
covered scars

She was so very
small, so very frail
Her filthy clothes,
her ragged nails

I could pick her up
with just one hand
She only crawled
could never stand

One day I took her
to the top of the stairs
In one hand I carried her
she was unawares

Right to the very top
from my one hand
I did drop

Let her fall
there at the very bottom.
Death came to gently
Swathe her in cotton.

Way out

I don't think I can face
yet another long winter
Another cold, dark morning
watching the ice splinter

Racing towards me
watching tiny cracks
come closer and closer
until at the bottom of the crevasse

I look around but there's
no clear path ahead
Surrounded by ice
surrounded by dread

Another problem
another worry
another stress
another flurry

of problems
blowing my way.
Another winter
of storm clouds
foreboding and grey.

The exit seems more distant
The light seems narrow

intermittent, flickering
swallowed up by shadow.

Frantically searching
for some way out
until ceasing to struggle
ceasing to shout

There's no more struggle with being
if no longer being am without
the interminable winter
then it's worth it, my way out.

What would you do

when all time has stopped?
What would you do
when the ground, it rocks?

What would you do
when your house has burnt down?
What would you do
when there's famine all around?

Tell me what you'd do
when your loved one has died?
Your world has been shattered
yet you're somehow still alive?

Even though it feels like your heart's been ripped wide
Can you tell me, tell me what you'd do?

You were well once

I was always wiling
away the time, whilst the washing was piling
babbling on whilst you were tidying
dinner's always served in perfect timing

Your voice like a song, you're the first one I'm dialling
when I'm far from home, I can almost hear you smiling
the other end of the line, your soul was shining

One day you were ill, can't stop mythering
It'll be gone in a few days, you keep reminding

Things got worse, but there was no reasoning
The doctors will sort it, but you were still weakening
Questioning why, the worry kept deepening
Troubling answers, fear started steepening

Hit with the truth. We're all left reeling
Set to explode, overwhelmed with feeling
It's your life, illness is stealing
This can't be the ending, fate's not sealing

Reality sets in, no amount of running
Can't escape from the chase, the constant drumming
is getting louder, the unthinkable is coming
no one can escape, the inevitable gunning

Can't you see that I'm trying, trying
to pretend it's okay, you're not really dying?
The façade is breaking, I'm no longer buying
consumed by my tears, I just end up crying

There's no hiding the truth, no point in lying
the dam's set to burst, my feelings are flying
spilling over the top, no point in sighing
can't stop you from falling, stop you from dying

Everyday things, like breathing and walking
are struggled triumphs, when death comes stalking
Your song has been silenced, there's no point in talking
there's nothing to say, when death's out hawking

My heart's in a vice, the beat is pounding
my stomach is sick, the fear is surrounding
my spirit is low, defeat is resounding
Nothing to comfort as death comes crowding

When will it end? I'm left wondering
My spirit is weak, my feet are stumbling
Wherever I turn I feel like I'm blundering
It's you who's dying, so why am I struggling?

You have been my rock, when the earth is rumbling

when the ground's giving way, the mountains
are tumbling
What can I do, when my rock is crumbling?
I can't carry on, I'm just left fumbling
for the words, the strength
I can't keep lumbering
on and on.
'Till death
finds you. Finally
Gone.

Friendship

Birthday message

I can't pretend to have gained much wisdom
in the extra months I've lived
Maybe you can at least avoid
the foolish things I did

Life's too short - you know that
so grab it each and every day
Remember to look around you
savour the small things along the way

Don't sit upon the side-lines
You're the author of your life
Time to kick the badass switch
and smash this thing called life

Know who your friends are
not the ones who just smile and say well done
but the people who surround you
pull you up, when you come undone

Listen closely to your heart
what's beating on the inside
It directs your path in life
don't push it to the side

Sometimes you'll feel awesome
you should do, don't be shy
But when you're feeling rubbish
don't be afraid to cry

It's just a sign you're human
We all need to show that sign
Always know where you can find a hug
to help you in that time

Sometimes the achievement
will be just getting out of bed
But for all the people who never tried
remember how far you are ahead

Sometimes it will feel like
the only way is down
Look up - there's an army of lifeboats
who refuse to let you drown

When you're on the rise again
let this feeling sink right in
Enjoy every drop of sunshine
let it get under your skin

No doubt you've already felt
the storms, the battering of this life
My words are no doubt far too late
to save you from much strife

Perhaps they are the things
I wish someone had written to me
a year or two ago, or three or four
would have helped to set me free

Today is *your* day though
to celebrate being alive
Look how far you've climbed already
time to watch you thrive

You're a bright young woman
with your whole long life ahead
Go show them what you're made of ...
It's time to knock 'em dead!

Burden

I wish I wasn't a burden
I can hear your inner sigh
I wish you weren't so good to me
then I'd stop questioning why

I wish I knew what to do
could plan the best way forward
I wish my ramblings on and on
didn't just leave you bored

I wish I knew how to help myself
so I didn't keep troubling you
I wish I could just work it out
instead of dragging you down too

Everyone needs help sometimes
I keep reminding myself
I just can't deal with things on my own
I really do need help

Every day feels like a mountain
every week a new peak
to climb, to struggle, to fall
I wish I wasn't just so weak

I'm fed up of wishing
I'm trying my very best
though every time I'm not good enough
I've failed another test

What's even more frustrating
I could never pay you back
that's not how kindness works
I know, but still I feel I lack

There's no possible way
that you could ever know
just how much you've helped me
by walking with me in my sorrow.

A compassionate friend

can blow away the sorrow
of my mind, remind me of happier times
when I feel so empty, so hollow

help me overcome my grief
please just sit with me, let me borrow
your hope of a better, brighter tomorrow.

Glimpse of a rainbow

You wrote for me a poem
I don't know what to say
You let me glimpse your rainbow
when everything felt so grey

You came with understanding
you know things weren't okay
you found me when I'm low
lifted me in your way

That only you could
with the gift of your words
to me it's not just a poem
it's a way of knowing I'm heard

And not alone,
that's the greatest gift there is
to not face the mountains alone
your kindness gives

So much support
there's so much I want to say
how grateful I am for the words
you wrote for me today

You don't need to build an island
or throw troubles in the sea
You just need to know
how much your kindness means to me.

Home

The night drifts by
as I lie
wide awake
my time I take
thinking of you
are you okay?

Your phone acts as a shield
Your brief text conceals
me knowing if you're alright
Is there something that might
betray a different story?
Your voice

falters and fades
as I watch the cascade
of tears down your face
as I try to replace
them with compassion and love
until they stop

I just need you to know this will end
in time your shattered soul will mend
I see the shards reflect in the light
even in the brokenness, beauty can find
itself sitting quietly, I see it

You think you were designed with a flaw
but I've been through so many of those doors
to your heart and have found nothing

but courage and kindness rushing
through boundless and strong
until silent

Your silence mends
your presence suspends
the pain, your quiet compassion
helps my grief unfasten
and yet
there are times

Your silence can hurt
What is worse
I want you to know how much I care
but the keys are locked to your lair
I bang on the door
and wait to be let in

You cry and lie awake
How long does it take
as I struggle to find the words
they escape like birds
from my mouth
and are lost

The phone does little to substitute for a hug
I would jump right through if only I could
Talk to me, find me, I'm waiting right here

I'll help you find the key
I'll lead you through the fear

We'll walk through this
together

You are not and could never be a bad person
I will not let you think that, I will not let it
worsen
You will not be the person that you were
and nothing could ever deter
me from finding you
where you are

Not where you think you ought to be
Not the person you think we should see
In the depths of depression
I make the confession
though I don't know how
we will find a way, I promise

That no matter where you are
whether near or far
from you, I'm on your side
I'll be your guide
I'll fight your fight
The darkest depths
will be uncovered
and the way out from the bottom
I promise you, will be discovered

You are not and never
have to go through this alone

I hope in my heart, in my hug
you can always find a home.

It's okay

to feel lost
It's okay to feel down
It's okay to need quiet
when you're out on the town

It's easier to hide
show them a smile
while the thoughts in your head
churn around all the while

It's okay to just sit
and have nothing to say
to just wish with a click
your problems go away

It's okay to struggle
It's okay to try
It's okay to fail
It's okay to just cry

I know you know
sometimes nothing
is okay. Okay is a lie
we hit on replay

I'm saying it's okay
because I've been there too
sometimes you just need
someone to listen to you

I know you don't want to burden
I get that too
but please don't cry alone
whatever you do

Wherever you are
whatever your pain
no matter how small
or silly, you pre-judge it to be vain

Feelings should be felt
have a right to be heard
so let them out
put them in words

Cry if you need to
let it all out
break something if you need to
yell, scream, shout

Whatever helps
whatever works for you
just please let me know
if there's anything I can do

Or not do
I can't promise to solve
but I can promise to listen, to care
though I can't dissolve

Or suddenly
magic anything away
I can be a friend
I hope that's okay

Tough is an understatement
to what life is
don't be afraid
of opening that lid

To your heart
the feelings inside
the doubts and the worries
the fears that reside

Don't wait for a lifeboat
without making a sign
it's hard for us to spot
if we can't see an outline

We all struggle sometimes
face a battle every day
I just want you to know
I'm here for you... okay? Xx

Meet up

-*Do you want to meet up?*-
Perhaps some other time.
~~When I can muster up the courage~~
~~to tell you I'm not fine~~

-*Don't you want to come out?*-
I'm just too tired to go.
~~Every day is a struggle~~
~~but I don't want you to know~~

-*Are you alright?*-
Yes everything's okay.
~~A pound for every lie~~
~~made ten quid today~~

-*Okay well maybe next time?*-
Yes that would be nice.
~~I've already said no once~~
~~I can't really say no twice~~

-*Did you bring your coat?*-
Yes I'm ready to go out.
~~Just push away reality~~
~~push away their doubt~~

-*It's good to see you smile!*-
~~I can even force a laugh.~~
~~Pretend I'm really happy~~
~~for yet another photograph~~

-Why aren't you telling me the truth?-
Because it's too much to bear.
~~If I bring it up, I'll break~~
~~I'll snag, then I'll just tear~~

-It's okay you know,
you're allowed to be upset-
Nothing is okay.
~~I can't escape her death~~

-What can I do to help?-
There's nothing to be done.
~~I can't change anything~~
~~Death's already won.~~

~~I don't always need help~~
~~sometimes just a friend~~
~~If you knew the truth~~
...Would you stay until the end?

Poetry

One day I met a girl
not much different from me
she had different hair and different eyes
but that's not what I could see

Her soul she kept inside
locked away with a key
but deeper down she knew
all she wanted was to be free

She wanted to be listened to
accepted and truly known
she wanted to find a kindred spirit
to find a heart she could make her home

Deep within her soul would dance
shimmering, shining bright
but she only ever let very few
close enough to see her light

Her words were wise, her thoughts were kind
she always made the time
to be a friend, to listen patiently
I heard a voice like mine

For although we were different
and had travelled different paths
we'd walked our different lives
yet had both our hearts a little cracked

Although she lived elsewhere
we met quite unexpectedly
friendship began to blossom
through our shared love of poetry

The rose

Lost and alone
in the darkest wood
where fears arise
and what could

Happen and what is
and what was
are lost underfoot
and what does

Become trampled
misunderstood
is hope. That
unopened bud

Claims on tomorrow
choked of joy
trapped in battle
our mind left to deploy

The sharpest arrows
against ourselves
our hearts become
where emotion swells

Reaching up
through toil and struggle
where light can be found
up out of the rubble

The rose that finds it way
through the cracks
that reaches through
the smallest gaps

Is not any less
beautiful
any less red
any less vibrant
or any more dead

The soil may be shallow
but the roots run deep
this is the promise
that friendship keeps

That there is always a way
of moving forwards
through every ravine
and every ford

The steepest mountain
can be climbed as ever
For we'll find a way
never alone
but always together.

Thank you

for listening to me
when nothing was okay
thank you for supporting me
when I couldn't do another day

Never underestimate
the power of a single kind deed
when all the world comes crashing down
a friend is all I need

I wouldn't have reached how far
I am, then from I where I was
I couldn't do it at all alone
but I kept going because

You kept the light on
you knew I'd be okay
even when I didn't know
you kept me from going astray

Thank you for caring
for reaching out a hand
when my feet were sinking
swallowed up in sand

When even the ground
is falling through
you didn't give up on me
so thank you

For helping me to breathe
when the air is running thin
and I don't even know
how or where to begin

To do another week
when another day was too much
thank you for having stayed
for keeping in touch

Thank you for every word
and thought and deed
thank you for being there
when I needed

Just a friend
just some company
just someone
who could really see me

enough to keep me going
enough to get me through
enough to get me to today
I couldn't get here without you.

The garden

A seed dropped in the ground
on the day we met
friendship grew a garden
that day I shan't forget

The lantern

In a room full of people
lost in the crowd
I'm sat here on my own
the silence is so loud

Why is it so painful?
Stop clawing at my scars
Don't you know how long it took
to build up this façade?

Just let me run away
Can't you see it now?
The tears I'm holding back
The worry in your brow

tells me you know
what's going on
sometimes I think
you are the only one

I don't have to speak
to say a single word
you're tuned in to my thoughts
you've clearly heard

each and every one
you whisper in my ear
you ask if I'm okay
you can see the unshed tear

I don't have to act
I don't have to pretend
you see me as I am
you accept me as a friend

Your compassion,
understanding
is parallel to none
even in the quiet
you gently carry me on

Without you I'd be lost
in a world of my own
you bring such light with you
wherever you are feels like home

When the world crumbles
when there's nothing left but smoke
you are my lantern
my flickering of hope

If I were to write an essay
or even a thousand books
if only to say thank you
it would never be enough

Even as I crumpled
inwardly collapsed
you took my hand
when all time had lapsed

When everything had faded
until there was nothing left
I know I can always hold
on to our friendship always kept

When the world stops turning
still it carries on
shining in the darkness
until all the darkness has gone.

Your voice

It wasn't that I left you
rather I was never there
never old enough or wise enough
to understand how I could care

For you properly
give you the help you need
fix your broken wings
give you the chance to succeed

I let you drown
I didn't even notice
how much you were struggling
how much you'd stopped floating

You'll say it's a two-way street
you could have spoken up too
but why did I leave all the hard parts,
leave everything down to you?

I didn't know how to help
the right things to say
I wasn't at the stage of my life
to help you find a way

I'm sorry for all the times I let you down
for all the things I left unsaid
for all the times I didn't speak
kept all the thoughts in my head

I'm sorry I wasn't stronger
wasn't helpful or wasn't kind
enough to see you suffer
and not leave you behind

I'm sorry I couldn't carry you
I just didn't know how
sorry isn't good enough
you've lost all those years now

I'm glad things are better
now I'm a bit more grown up
at least I hope I am
I hope I can fill up your cup

With each and every deed
keep it nicely above half full
I hope to give you happiness
to stray away from me being dull

You deserve to be happy
you deserve to have fun
now I've worked out how
I've only just begun

You deserved to be loved
you deserve to know your worth
you deserve to know
how much you mean to me
you're the best friend on this earth

I'm not great for helping you
I'm not kind for opening my eyes
I'm not amazing for letting you shine
I'm not awesome for giving you a surprise

You are great because of YOU
so much kindness in your eyes
you are amazing to watch you shine
you are awesome just being alive

You don't have to thank me
for doing anything at all
it's nothing to what you've given me
what I've helped with is so small

Don't be afraid to stand up. Stand tall
make yourself known
remember when you stand
you'll never stand alone

Speak up. Write up
say it out loud
I'm proud of you already
it's time to make yourself proud

This is your life
this is your time
this is your chance
to make the climb

Keep being bold
keep making a courageous choice
this is your year
now it's time to find your voice.

Goodbye

The last goodbye

Would you recognise me now
if I passed you in the street?
On the outside much the same
but on the inside much more complete

Would you recognise the confidence
the self-esteem in each step?
The way I look forward
keep on going without regret?

Without doubting who I am
all the choices that I make?
Could you foresee who I'd become
the steps you wouldn't watch me take?

Where I ought to go
when you knew me back then
Would you believe how I would grow
did you know even back then?

Would you be proud of me now
the woman I've become?
If I turned out only half as kind
then my job would be well done

Do I have your patience?
I'm afraid I don't
I've tried to be as good
but I know that I won't

Would I be as fierce
in protecting those I love?
I tried to protect you
the very best that I could

Would I be as resilient
through all the challenges you faced?
I didn't think I could
your love could not erase

My weakness, the times
I wanted to give up
when each step was too difficult
still you'd lift me up

When your feet were falling
when there was no other way
when you had to leave us
it was selfish begging you to stay

Do I carry your compassion
could I match you by half?
You never stopped giving
bringing your light to the dark

Could I be as faithful
as you were to me?
The years have been snatched
for me to prove that I would be

What would you think
if you're looking from above?
I hope I'd do you justice
I hope you'd think that I was good

I'm sorry for all the times
I could have done more
I could have been stronger
I should have been before

You left us before our time
should have run out
I keep on writing to you
but you're just never about

Anymore
and it's difficult to know
that I'll never get an answer
you've gone somewhere I can't go

All these unsaid words
I'll never get one more reply
all I have is memories
all that's left, our last goodbye.

The promise

Nothing is ever enough
keep on running, but can't stand up

Chasm between us, a life-time wide
can't seem to cross, to the other side

Every minute, every day
never knowing if things will be okay

When every day feels like a year
all that time has disappeared

Every week, looking back
holding on to something cracked

Every month, a deeper scar
no matter how far I run, I'm never far

All that grief, all that pain
comes rushing back, like a hurricane

Need to rest from this race
hope everything will fall into place

You were my world and now you're gone
how was I meant to just move on?

Tell me how, when it's been a year
there's a lifetime left without you here?

I loved you more than I thought I could
I haven't stopped and I never would

I get told I'm doing well
but it all feels false, can never tell

If perhaps it was all a dream
you left for a while but one day you'll be

Right here, sat next to me
only in death will be set free

To sit with you again
like we did, when we were best friends

My anchor, mentor, my constant guide
you weren't supposed to leave my side

You were everything and more to me
now you're gone, and I can't see

The way ahead, the world's painted black
the way out of here long since lost track

They say you're up there, looking down
if I believed that I'd be in the ground

Just to spend another minute with you
eternity there, mustn't be true

If only I could turn the hands of time
take things back to when you were mine

When the best thing we had was each other
it's been a year but I still can't recover

After all this time, has anything changed?
Fearing the memories will start to fade

All I have of you in photographs
how can they hold the love I can't get back?

This, the first of many years to come
will I still write to you, like I have done?

Will it hurt as much every time
a milestone is passed, at every sign?

All those moments you should have been there
will it ever make sense, or stop feeling unfair?

Promise me I can always talk to you
I know you can't answer, but it's all I can do

Promise me you'll keep in touch
with my heart, with my mind, don't say it's too much

I never left you and I never will
promise me you'll be here with me still

I love you more than you could ever know
but if you can make just one promise
Promise me you won't ever let me go.

You're asleep now

resting quietly
Sometimes
a gentle rest
yet sometimes
a bitter test

To hear you struggle
to breathe
Take a breath
real slow
Please take another one
Please don't go

It's okay
if you want to
if you need to be free
But I'm still
not quite yet ready
for you to give up
on me.

Reflection

Christmas

The planning you won't do
Christmas cards you won't write
the gifts not secretly wrapped
nor hidden out of sight

The cards won't be hung up
crackers won't be cracked
no presents to exchange
no one dares to have laughed

The Christmas dinner you won't cook
and painstakingly prepare
all the things you won't do
because you won't be there

It's supposed to be a time
to spend with family sharing love
but the only way I can see you
is if your grave I've dug

Like a bauble that is broken
our family no longer whole
Christmas has been stolen
without you it has no soul

Just empty like a shadow
of everything that was
A flickering memory
is all we have because

You are gone
and you're never coming back
you took with you the joy
of a season now painted black

With sorrow
happiness stripped bare
you had made us a family
sat by the fire in your chair

You were the fire
the hearth of our home
in you our heart was kept
but now the fire has blown

out. Extinguished.
There's nothing that remains
but ash and smoked out memories
as we fight to keep the flame

So, whilst the rest of the world
looks forward to Christmas day
I'll just close my eyes and wish
that day to go away.

It's mum's birthday today

No picking out the nicest card in the shop
finding the loveliest bouquet, where no petals
had dropped

Searching for unopened buds for longer display
mum's favourite chocolates, hidden away

All in preparation for her special day
not so much big, for she was quiet that way

No such preparations, yet momentous in its own way
for the first time she's resting, without us
and without us she'll stay.

Long after the flowers had drooped

and started to look sad
all the leaves had fallen away
the brightest blooms had flagged

Long after the sympathy cards
had left the mantelpiece
thinking of you had left the lips
Is there anything I can do? - had ceased

Long after the funeral
the days and weeks that passed
the months and years that had fallen away
the only thing that would last

Was the hole that grew and grew
as she had begun to die
all the tears I'd kept hidden
just didn't want to dry

The emptiness she'd left behind
the hole that never shrank
where I'd long for her embrace
where all my tears they sank

Perhaps one day when all is done
when there's no more tears to cry
I think I'll finally rest with her
where she'll never leave my side.

Sorry for your loss

Just wanted to say
I'm sorry for your loss
Thanks. A small smile
a chance to gloss

Over grief, no one knows
what to say
too afraid to speak
so they simply walk away

Alone a tear falls
like the first drop upon a leaf
before the downpour of the storm
the outpouring of grief

Sometimes it would help
for another outlet to flow
other than the heart
where all the sorrow grows

Maybe a tree whose roots
are large and strong
under whose leaves can find shelter
in whose branches can belong

At a time when no one
knows just what to say
to put roots into my pain
and to simply stay

To bear with
to simply be present
is the most valued gift
gained from grief's bitter lesson.

The Joker

I met an ordinary man
to me it seemed anyway
he was pleasant and polite
whilst going about his day

Sometimes he laughed when wasn't happy
he cried when wasn't sad
he masked his emotions
he tried not to be bad

He hurt on the inside
too dark and deep to know
he masked his pain in comedy
he put on a great show

He tried to be good
they simply jeered and laughed
he had his minute of fame
his pictures autographed

They stopped him in the street
then kicked him to the floor
they stole all his money
they left him weak and poor

He tried to reach out
but received no sign of help
in the end he realised
he only had himself

His mother he did love
he worshipped and he cared
when she began to suffer
he made himself prepared

He knew the only way
was to take away the pain
take away all that hurt
to make things right again

Failed by society
those dark thoughts in his mind
no one to tame his emotions
no one in which to confide

Powerless, helpless
one day he lashed out
their bodies lay in pieces
Did you ever doubt

violence could be the answer
to those thoughts that exist?
that lie deep inside
that we pretend we've missed

He finally felt something
instead of numbness inside
it was only by taking a life
he finally felt alive

Now finally free
perhaps I take his side
why do I sympathise far more with him
than all those who've died?

When someone gets killed
murderous acts we scorn
Can we still pass judgment
even if killers aren't really born?

They are made
when we decide to look away
from the pleasant, ordinary man
who suffers quietly every day.

Unexpected friend

From afar, a stranger in the distance
I spot him.
The other side of the street
someone we don't get to meet
Perhaps another house
in another place
a familiar face
but never to us.

Now I see him more clearly
He lived on the fringes before
but then he opened the door
and now he's moved in.

Most people are frightened of him
but they don't understand
he's got everything planned.

He helps those who are suffering
He comforts and lets them rest
He gives them a final test
then puts them at ease

Bringing calm and certainty
even welcome relief
when we're too upset to speak
he takes away the pain
makes things right again

Most unexpectedly of course
he has become closer to us
He never made a fuss
just quietly became
a part of our family.

Closer and closer
till the very end
The day that Death
became our friend.

Wanting

I've given up wanting to be happy
think I'll settle with okay
Okay is not stressed or worried
is calmly facing the day

I'd wanted a fresh new start
try to turn over a new leaf
But how could I forget you?
Would be like forgetting to breathe

I'd wanted to linger in sadness
How could I possibly move on?
My world had just stopped turning
The person I loved the most had gone

I'd wanted everyone else to be upset
How could they go about their day?
Their lives so happy and normal
I wished them all to go away

Didn't think I wanted everyone's pity
to feel the depths of my despair
but I wanted someone to grieve with me
to have someone in which to share

I wanted to have time alone
so I could be left to cry
Yet I felt all the more lost
under tear-stained sheets I did lie

I wanted to have a friend
to just be given a hug
to be held until I stop crying
to feel my mother's love

I wanted to hear her voice
for just one more time
I wanted to see her smile
take her hand in mine

I wanted to tell her I loved her
and I still very much do
She is still my world
my anchor I cling onto

I wanted her to be with me
and I know that she still is
I knew she would never leave me
here in my heart, she'll always live.

The Journey

Bloom again

All day long we take and take
'till desolate lands do we make
Nature lost, earth plundered
far from our homes we wandered

Into lands strange and new
where creatures roamed
and forests grew

Everything seen, everything found
from far above, deep underground
We extracted, exploited and we thieved
whilst the earth was left to grieve

Nature left alone to cry, as its glory began to die
the earth we so relied upon
All its riches long since gone

Without the earth to sustain
people could not long remain
and now without human blight
Nature will no longer fight

For as long as sun and rain remain
the Earth will one day bloom again.

Final journey

For some, the roads had been too long
the paths too overgrown
the winds too fierce and strong
the exit blocked with stone

The journey too prolonged
'till we reached the final depths
where we laid our aching bones
we laid them out to rest.

Found

A compass with no arrow
a map without a key
a place without a name
that's where you'll find me

I've been lost for so long
seasons all lost track
been wandering on and on
given up finding a way back

Until a voice broke the silence
an arrow sliced the air
a key dropped in my hand
I became aware

Of where I was
the path beneath my feet
the lantern flickered on
I found I was in my street

Where I'd lived
where I'd been all this time
home had not been home
there had been no sign

I recognised it now
the warmth reaching out
Winter had arrived
but the flame was lit no doubt

As the fire crackled gently
shared its friendly glow
gathered round the faces
of all those I love and know

I never needed a compass
or a map when gone astray
all I needed was a friend
to help me find the way

After so long of waiting
in the silence that surrounds
the distance impossible
yet here you are, I'm found.

Hopeful eyes

As in spring a leaf uncurled
innocent tender bud unfurled
those hopeful eyes upon the world

Rose tinted glasses full of wonder
before can even think to blunder
Spell of life they're still under

Yet we are full of too much worry
fretful, concerned, thoughts in a hurry
listening to our inner bully

To avoid making any wrong turns
second guess ourselves, confidence burns
childhood freedom soon unlearned

Can't be seen to step outside
so all our thoughts we try to hide
against the critics, their forces wide

Their shouts, their imposed reality
pushing in favour of herd mentality
foisted upon us, no more individuality
Refuse to be crushed,
let's war against insanity

Let's stand up, not just take a seat
fight for the world, we want to meet
the boundless opportunities there used to be
when we could view things properly
just tiny people with tiny feet
tiny hands and tiny heartbeat.

I can't explain

the problem of evil
the colour of the sky
the flight of an eagle

What is time?
How big is space?
Where do I fit
in this awfully big place?

Why do we lose
those that we love?
Is it the working
of hands from above?

Why do we mourn
those that are lost?
As though they are gone
lines cannot be uncrossed

Their love endures
in the heart it does not fade
though the body dies
Love finds a way
to always survive.

Oceans blue

Sometimes I sigh
as a mountain looms ahead
But then I change perspective
the hill brings far less dread

Sometimes I'm anxious
Rapids drawing near
It's only a small stretch
until the water's calm and clear

Sometimes I worry
approaching the waterfall
But none of us knows
what really lies in store

Sometimes I fear
the river reaching its end
But there's just another turn
it weaves another bend

In the end you'll realise
the destination didn't matter
The journey was what counted
still reaching the ocean thereafter

Where everyone is heading
who knows what lies beneath
I'm not afraid of finding out
what mysteries lie in the deep

I've tumbled over boulders
I've fought to swim upstream
I've burst my banks time and again
crashed through every ravine

Every stone I've worn away
has worn away me too
until there's no more left to break
I'll rest finally in oceans blue

The nest

There was a bird
who soared in the sky
far above the rest
so very high

and distant
so far out of reach
for others to join her
yet they would all speak

of her power
her strength and her grace
but none of them got close enough
to ever see her face

She flew every day
watched over her young
protected them with her life
safe where they belonged

One day she flew
too far from the nest
in search of food
too far to protect

her children
and so one by one
she took her revenge
on those who had done

this to her
who had taken her beloved
She tried to stay strong
She tried to stay good

But she couldn't fight
the rage that tore her soul
destroyed from the inside
until no longer whole

So she stopped flying
she stopped being seen
she stopped wishing
for everything that had been

to return
to come rushing back
She tried to live with her scars
still burned on her back

She couldn't live like this
hurting every day
Every hour, every minute
it needed to go away

So she soared one last time
up to the sky
then plummeted downwards
where she would lie

with her children
She had made a new nest
She would always be with them
She could finally rest

They were together
now in death, as in life
Just as she had hoped for
she'd done everything right

She had been a mother
and hadn't she loved?
Hadn't she provided?
Hadn't she done enough?

She could rest peacefully
nothing could sever
she was still their mother
and would be forever.

The scene

The scene is set
The actors are waiting
I'm the only one not knowing
the role that they're playing

I'm a master of disguise
when pretending I'm okay
A torrent of emotions
washes the mask away

I'm weak for having tried
when it's never good enough
I'm a fool for having lied
denying things are tough

I've tried to play the hero
by not asking for help
I've tried to walk alone
think I can do it all myself

Like climbing up a mountain
with a boulder on my back
or trying to go up backwards
everyone just laughs

Another battle lost
another hundred plagues
disaster befalls me
chaos fills the stage

It wouldn't be so bad
if I could only skip a scene
skip an act or two
find it was only just a dream

I'm tired of trying to play
all these different parts
whilst the roof is caving in
I'm being pelted at by darts

It's all a bit dramatic
but what I'm really trying to say
I can't just drop the act
when my whole life is a play.

The test

They said it was a test
I sat down like all the rest
I crawled, I stood, I ran
I thought I had a plan

Some kind of endurance test
Sometimes I just guessed
what to do, not get it wrong
it was just so awfully long

Sometimes we had breaks
sometimes I would awake
I forgot I was still being tested
didn't do what they suggested

Twenty positions back
they cut me no slack
I'd returned, dropped behind
the end was never clarified

It was a race we didn't want to run
it was only when nearly done
once we knew the finish line
was the end of our time

Our clock had finally stopped
the end was now unlocked
Finally cut with a knife
slashed the finish line to this life.

Beyond

Always

Scrolling my phone
to pass the time
Distract my mind I find
myself
lost
alone
disconnected
unprotected
overwhelmed

I stay quiet
don't want to burden
try to hide
I'm so uncertain

Blackness and smoke
I start to choke
on hopelessness and despair
she's no longer there

Can't contain the flame
now just ashes remain
The life that was
and just because
it came
doesn't mean
it can't go
but we all know the ending.
Stop pretending.

Why must you suffer so much?
Already such
loss and pain
Losing you already
all hope in vain
bit by bit
part by part
It can take your body
but please not your heart

If there was a way
to take away the pain
I would do anything
to make you well again

If only I had the power
to turn the days
into weeks
the minutes
into hours

When everything is taken
until all we have left
is each other
I'll *always* be your daughter
You'll *always* be my mother.

Enough

Alone on my bed
with the demons in my head
whilst in the comfort of my home
I can feel so alone
falling prey to the lie
I'm not good enough

Feeding off low self-esteem
any confidence wiped clean
surrounded by negative thoughts
as though I had been taught
no matter what you do
you're not good enough

Falling deeper in despair
no one around to be there
when things are never what they seem
and I can only dream
of sometime, somehow, please now
being good enough

Feeling so trapped inside
like you always have to hide
Waiting for the day
for someone to say
I believe in you
you are enough

But being afraid to speak
I remained weak kept others far away
for fear of having them stay
close enough to know
I'm not good enough

One day I'd had enough
of feeling low when things were rough
I decided to let someone in
into the dark, into the dim
for me to escape my prison
of not being enough

As though I'd been let down a rope
I gained heart, I gained hope
from the demons in the night
to the hope of the light
they believed I was worth saving
that I was enough

Looking back, I'm so grateful
but sometimes I'm still hateful
of who I was, who I am
All the regrets that I have
still trying to believe
I am good enough

But when I begin to believe in me
and the person who I can be
then I will truly be set free
to truly believe
I am more than enough

But that day is yet to come
for the journey isn't done
But though I still lose my way
for now, for today
with the demons kept at bay
I believe I can say, with certainty
honesty and courage... *I am enough.*

Love that never breaks

You have taught me so much
always led by example
pouring out selflessness, love
shining bright as a candle

No matter how dark the path
you have always lit the way
held me up, held me strong
never gone astray

You have listened patiently
and always with care
Gentle yet strong
firm and yet fair

You make me feel valued
and always respected
important and cherished
never once neglected

Wise, considerate, thoughtful
counsel for my woes
a balm for my troubles
took the thorns from my rose

Just so that I would be safe
you sacrificed so much
just to raise me up
I'll never forget the touch

Of your hand
the warmth of your smile
brighter than a thousand lanterns
and all the while

Your body faded
lacked strength to stand
you poured out your love
with just a touch of your hand

Your embrace is one
to light up my soul
to strengthen my spirit
and make me feel whole

A thousand words
could never do justice
to the depth of your love
I may never again hold your hand
or be held in a hug

But I feel it course through me
every breath that I take
you are always with me
a love that never breaks.

Midnight star

You are the star
in the midnight sky
The North in my compass
when I'm questioning why

The oasis in my desert
when even tears run dry
I'll love you, always love you
love you 'till I die.

My everything

You have laid down your traps
and taken *everything* that was good

You have come here with your weapons
and taken *everything* I have loved

You took the sun out the sky
then laughed as I froze

You were too busy sneering
to watch me as I rose

You think you can take *everything*
when you're twisting in the knife

You're forgetting that my *everything*
is the one who gave me life

You can't take my *everything*
when she's not yours to take

She's made of something stronger
something you can't break

You hold no power over us
no matter how you tug

For nothing, not even death
can ever break a mother's love.

Peace

There is peace to be found
in the quiet evening air
in the empty bed
the still empty chair

She would have enjoyed
the soft bird song
on the warm breeze
the shadows cast long

Her gentle smile
as the sun upon her face
set itself gently
took her to a better place.

Heaven

is a place
where she is waiting for me
like a boat finding harbour
seeking shelter from the sea

Heaven is a place
where she calls out my name
as a lighthouse signals home
for ships tossed by wind and rain

Heaven is a place
that I can no longer reach
her soft voice disappears
like sand swept across the beach

Memories just like driftwood
come floating back on the tide
except they're hollowed out and
broken, charred upon all sides

An ocean lies between us
no one dares to go as deep
she remains forever lost
in the endlessness of sleep

Heaven is a place
now so very far away
it used to be right here
but she simply couldn't stay

She had to make a place
out in the unknown
so when my own time comes
I'll already have a home

That's the only reason why
I could think that she left
but if I met her now
she wouldn't want to see me yet

To keep me from going early
she left me a small piece
of heaven as a reminder
for which I'll forever keep

No storm can break her anchor
no matter how fierce the wave
nothing can break the bond between us
that triumphs even over the grave

Heaven is not a place
I need to travel to
she is always with me
in everything I see and do

Death, where is your victory?
Though I have felt your sting
you have not destroyed me
for I'm rising on the wind

There's nothing left to fear
not even death stands in my way
You think I'll just stay broken?
When she's with me every day

Heaven is lost and found
Can you see it through my eyes?
No matter how many times I may fall
and even still I'll rise

The only thing I know for certain
when no-one knows what lies above
Death can only take life
But it can *never* take away love.

The End

Thank you for reading to the end of this book. I know that for many, the path through grief does not end in peace, if indeed the path ends at all. It is more of a journey and peace I hope is a place you can pass through. It is rather many twists and turns, and you may find yourself back at the same place or stuck with the same feeling many, many times. I can't tell you when things may start to feel better or that they won't feel worse again. I can only say that I have found talking to others – reaching out to friends, family, colleagues – whoever you trust that is in your circle – that it can help.

Writing thoughts down can also help when you're not able or don't feel up to talking to someone. Poetry has of course been immensely healing for me. Both writing my own and reading/hearing others' poems. But any form of expression, of letting those feelings out, as long as you're doing no one any harm – it can help.

I hope this book will be a small reminder that you are not alone and that you don't have to face things alone either. A small reminder that death can only take life, but it cannot take away love. No one can take that from you. You will find a way to carry that love with you always. As difficult as it may be. As much as you may feel you can't go on.

We must try to find a way to carry on, by keeping those we love always in our hearts. Even though they may be fit to break.

Love cannot be broken.

Keep going. Dare to ask for help, to let someone you trust know how you feel. You are not alone. Sending you my love,

Beth xxx

Printed in Great Britain
by Amazon